The Clubhouse Game Book

Sterling Publishing Co., Inc.
New York

Library of Congress Cataloging-in-Publication Data

10 9 8 7 6 5 4 3 2 1

The Secret Club House game book / Jim Sukach ... [et al.] ; illustrated by
Lucy Corvino ... [et al.].
    p. cm.
  Includes index.
  ISBN 1-4027-1107-7
  1. Games—Juvenile literature. 2. Puzzles--Juvenile literature. [1. Word games. 2.
  Games. 3. Puzzles.] I. Sukach, Jim. II. Corvino, Lucy, ill.
  GV1203.S443 2004
  793.73—dc22

                                                                    2003024878

Published by Sterling Publishing Co., Inc.
387 Park Avenue South, New York, NY 10016
© 2004 by Sterling Publishing Co., Inc.

Debra Spina Dixon, Illustrator
Excerpted from *Quicksolve Whodunit Puzzles* © 1995 by Jim Sukach; *Clever
Quicksolve Whodunit Puzzles* © 1999 by Jim Sukach; *Loony Laws and Silly Statutes* ©
1994 by Sheryl Lindsell-Roberts; Illustrations © 1994 by Myron Miller; *Funny Laws
and Other Zany Stuff* © 1999 by Sheryl Lindsell-Roberts; *Quick-to-Solve Brainteasers*
© 1996 and 1967 in Argentina and Spain by Juegos & Co., S.R.L., and Zugarto
Ediciones under the titles *Para Resolver en el Autobus and Para Resolver en el
Ascensor*; *Hard-to-Solve Brainteasers* © 1978 and 1996 in Argentina and Spain by
Juegos & Co., S.R.L., and Zugarto Ediciones under the title *Como Jugar y Divertirse
con su Inteligencia*; *Challenging Math Puzzles* © 1997 by Glen Vecchione; *The Little
Giant Book of Math Puzzles* © 2000 by Derrick Niederman; *Dr. Knock-Knock's Official
Knock-Knock Dictionary* © 1976 by Joseph Rosenbloom; *The Little Giant Book of
Science Experiments* © 1998 by Sterling Publishing Co., Inc., published by
Ravensburger Buchverlag Otto Maier GmbH under the titles *Spiel—das Wissenschaft*
© 1964, 1995; *Der Natur auf der Spur* © 1972, 1995; *Geheimnisse des Altags* © 1977,
1995; *Easy Magic Tricks* © 1994 by Bob Longe; *The Little Giant Book of Magic Tricks* ©
2002 by Bob Longe; *Secret Hiding Places (for Clever Kids)* © 2001 by Mark Shulman;
illustrations © 2001 by Annie Galvin; *Cartooning for Kids* © 2001 by Mike Artell; *Get
Out!* © 2001 Orange Avenue, Inc; *Zany Rainy Days* © 2000 Hallie Warshaw.
Distributed in Canada by Sterling Publishing
^c/o Canadian Manda Group, One Atlantic Avenue, Suite 105
Toronto, Ontario, Canada M6K 3E7
Distributed in Great Britain and Europe by Chris Lloyd at Orca Book
Services, Stanley House, Fleets Lane, Poole BH15 3AJ, England
Distributed in Australia by Capricorn Link (Australia) Pty. Ltd.
P.O. Box 704, Windsor, NSW 2756, Australia

Sterling ISBN 1-4027-1107-7

Contents

Quicksolve Whodunits

Dr. Jeffrey Lynn Quicksolve, professor of criminology, retired from the police force as a detective at a very young age. Now he works with various police departments and private detectives as a consultant when he is not teaching at the university.

He certainly knows his business, solving crimes. Many people are amazed at how he solves so many crimes so quickly. When asked how he does it, he replies, "I'm no smarter than anyone else. I just listen very well."

Read, listen, think carefully, and you can solve these crimes too.

Solutions on page 123.

Jilted Joker

"We're stumped," Officer Longshot said to Dr. J. L. Quicksolve. "This should be an open-and-shut case. We've got a suspect at the scene. We've got a motive. But we've got no weapon!"

"Tell me the whole story," Dr. Quicksolve said.

"A man was murdered at the circus. He was a trapeze artist. Our suspect is a clown who was jilted by one of the women who ride the elephants. Apparently, she jilted the clown for this trapeze guy. The clown was jealous and shot him behind one of the circus trucks," Officer Longshot explained.

"You said the clown was caught at the scene?" Dr. Quicksolve asked.

"Yes, he was seen selling balloons a few minutes before a shot was heard. A couple of people looked behind the wagon and found the clown standing next to the body. The guy was shot with a small caliber pistol, probably a derringer, but we can't find it. The people who found him said the clown didn't have anything at all. We searched him at the scene—nothing. We got out the dogs to search for the weapon. We even looked up on top of the truck but we just can't find the gun. There's no way, as far as I can see, that he could have gotten rid of the gun. We'll have to let him go."

"Maybe the gun was a little farther away than you could see, by the time you got there," Quicksolve said.

What did Dr. Quicksolve mean?

Skating Rink Robbery

Dr. Quicksolve entered the skating rink building. You could hear the loud music they played, even in the lobby. In the main room where the people were skating around and around, you could hardly carry on a conversation because of the loud music.

The manager, Mr. Blade, came over to the detective and signaled for him to come through a nearby door marked "Office." When they went in and closed the door, you couldn't hear the music, and they could talk. Two men were sitting in the office. One was holding an ice pack to his head.

"I had this room made soundproof to keep out the loud music the teenagers like so much. The problem is, we've been robbed. I just got here myself, so I'll let my employees, Frank and Joe, tell you what happened. Joe, you go first."

The one with the ice pack spoke up. "I was in here counting the money. I was sitting here with my back to the door and someone came in behind me and hit me over the head. When I came to, the money was gone."

"What can you tell us?" Dr. Quicksolve asked, turning toward Frank.

"I was out in the main room watching the skaters. I heard a crash from the office here, and I turned around just in time to see a tall man slip out of the office and run out of the building. I came in and found Joe unconscious. I woke him and called the police."

"So where did you hide the money so quickly, Frank?" Dr. Quicksolve asked.

Why did Dr. Quicksolve suspect Frank?

Burglars and Bludgeons

Dr. J. L. Quicksolve drove straight down the main road out of town for 20 miles before he got to the only turn he would make to reach Sara and Will Bludgeon's cabin north of the city. Beyond this was 40 miles of wilderness. He drove a quarter mile through the dense woods before he reached the cabin. Three police officers were there waiting for him.

After greetings were exchanged, Officer Longshot explained, "Mrs. Bludgeon has been murdered. She was struck on the head with a blunt object, apparently by a burglar. Will Bludgeon, her husband, said he was upstairs in the shower when he heard his wife scream. He raced downstairs and found his wife lying dead in the family room. The burglar was gone."

"Did he call the police immediately, then?" asked Dr. Quicksolve.

"No, they don't have a telephone hooked up way out here in the woods. He was stopped by these officers for speeding just north of here. He said he was in a hurry to get help and to report the burglary and murder. They called us on their police radio," Officer Longshot said.

Dr. Quicksolve looked around the cabin and examined the broken back door. Finally, he turned to Officer Longshot and said, "Hold Will Bludgeon on suspicion of murdering his wife. There was no burglar."

Why does Dr. Quicksolve think Will Bludgeon
killed his own wife?

Smith and Smith, Ex-Partners

There were two partners in the law firm of Smith and Smith. They were not brothers. One of them was dead. His body was by his partner in his partner's house. Dr. J. L. Quicksolve was having lunch with his friend Sergeant Rebekah Shurshot, discussing a case, when she got the call on her portable receiver. They were at Mr. Smith's house in a matter of minutes, in spite of the traffic and rainy weather.

They hurried up to the door and were let in out of the rain by one of two officers who had gotten there just ahead of them. Mr. Smith was sitting at the kitchen table. The body of the other Mr. Smith lay covered nearby.

The back door that led to the backyard had obviously been jimmied with a knife. There was water on the floor, probably tracked in by the killer.

Mr. Smith was explaining, "My partner, John, was here to meet me to talk over business. We had planned to meet here and I left the front door unlocked in case he got here first. Apparently he did, and he was sitting here when someone broke in through the back door and stabbed him. I parked my car in the garage and came in through the side door there from the garage. The killer probably heard me coming and went out this back door when he heard me drive into the garage. I'm glad I didn't walk in on a killer with a knife!"

"Well," said Dr. Quicksolve, looking under the table.

Why was he looking under the table?

Made in the Shades

"He was about six feet tall. He had brown hair, blue eyes, and a small scar on his left cheek." The clerk of the small country store was describing the man she said had robbed the store earlier that morning.

Standing there beside Dr. J. L. Quicksolve was Sergeant Rebekah Shurshot, who said, "Tell us exactly what happened, step- by- step."

"Well, this guy came in the door there. He went to that rack of sunglasses over there by the door and he tried on several pairs while I waited on a couple of other customers: a lady buying a magazine and a boy buying candy. When no one else was in the store, he came over with a pair of the sunglasses on, and asked me how they looked. I said they looked good. Then he said he would take them and a pack of cigarettes. When I turned my back to get the cigarettes, he pulled out a gun, and he said it was a stickup. He said to give him the money, so I did. Then he ran out and got into a blue car. I wasn't able to get the license, but he drove out the drive and then west. That's when I called the police," the clerk told them.

"There seems to be one flaw in this story," Dr. Quicksolve said.

What was wrong with the story?

Postal Clown

The one small lamp in the dark living room cast shadows that added to the eerie feeling of evil as the flickering fire gave only short glimpses of the two outlines on the floor. Tape on the carpet marked where the two bodies had lain. A dark stain spread across the carpet.

"Plunder and Pillage," Sergeant Rebekah Shurshot told Dr. J. L. Quicksolve. "It looks like they were killed with an axe. IRS agents—apparently they were here to question our suspect, Soapy Waters, about his tax returns."

"Soapy Waters?" Dr. Quicksolve asked.

"That's not his real name. It's what he calls himself when he's working as a clown. He does charity things—parades and stuff. He walks around on stilts, squirting people with a huge squirt gun. He's really a postal worker. He's on medical leave right now," Sergeant Shurshot said.

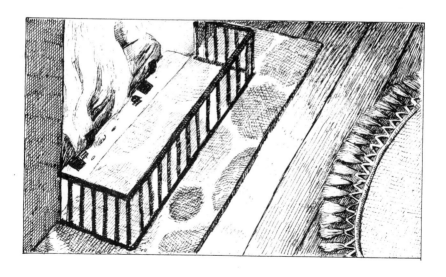

"His alibi?" Dr. Quicksolve asked.

"He said he was upstairs sleeping with the radio on. He thinks they came right in because they heard the radio. He said his neighbor, Lizzy Borden, must have come over to complain about his music, lost her temper, and killed the two IRS men. He pointed out the tracks in the snow," Sergeant Shurshot said, looking out the window at tracks leading from the only house nearby. They showed small footprints in the snow going in each direction, back and forth.

"They are—" Dr. Quicksolve began.

"Too small to be his," Sergeant Shurshot said. "Should I go get Miss Borden for questioning?"

"Let's look around here for a couple of things first," Dr. Quicksolve said.

What did Dr. Quicksolve want to find?

Dit Dah Dilemma

Dr. Quicksolve arrived at the scene just as the ambulance pulled away. "Thomas Graff," said Officer Longshot, as Dr. Quicksolve approached. "He's unconscious. The medics say it looks like a coma. He may or may not recover, they said. He was struck by a bullet in the head some time early this morning. He was found lying here in the parking lot in front of his office about an hour ago."

"Who found him?" Dr. Quicksolve asked.

"His partner, Sam Morris, found him lying here when he came in to work about seven o'clock this morning," Officer Longshot explained.

"Did Mr. Graff say anything to his partner or anyone before he became unconscious?"

"No, but he apparently tried to write a message here in the dirt. I guess he was too weak to tell what he was doing. It's just scratches, lines in the dirt."

Dr. Quicksolve looked at the marks etched in the ground. They were just lines—some short, some longer. There were three short lines, then a short and a longer line, followed by two longer lines—no legible words.

"Be sure Mr. Graff has an officer with him in the hospital, and bring Mr. Morris in for questioning," Dr. Quicksolve directed.

Why bring in Sam Morris?

Funny Laws

Remember the old joke, "Why did the chicken cross the road (to get to the other side)?" Well, believe it or not, there are laws on the books against a chicken crossing the road (in Quitman, Georgia), disturbing your neighbors by snoring (in Dunn, North Carolina), and breaking more than three dishes a day (in Florida). In Sweden it's illegal to train your seal to balance a ball on its nose. In Iceland, anybody can practice medicine, as long as he or she hangs out a sign that reads "Quack Doctor." And in France in the 1950s, it was illegal to land a flying saucer in the vineyards (it's okay now).

Some of these laws have been modernized. Some are just hanging around, and others are out-and-out bloopers. For example, in Kansas: "When two trains approach each other at a crossing, both shall come to a full stop and neither shall start up until the other has gone." It's quite possible that some of these laws have been repealed in recent years. But they've probably been replaced by new laws that will seem as ridiculous to future generations as these do to us!

Laws for Drivers

In Tennessee, you cannot drive a car while you are asleep.

In Cleveland, Ohio, you cannot operate any motor vehicle while sitting in someone's lap.

In Macomb, Illinois, it is illegal for an auto to impersonate a wolf.

In Minneapolis, anyone who double-parks an auto shall be put on a chain gang and fed bread and water.

In Milwaukee, a motorist cannot park an auto for more than two hours unless hitched to a horse.

In Glendale, Arizona, a car is forbidden to back up.

In Rutland, Vermont, your car is forbidden to backfire.

In San Francisco, you'd better not get caught wiping your car with used underwear. It's unlawful.

It is illegal in the state of Florida to transport livestock aboard school buses.

In Youngstown, Ohio, it's illegal to ride on the roof of a taxi.

In Albuquerque, New Mexico, it is forbidden to reach out and pull prospective passengers into the cab.

In Florida, anyone found underneath the sidewalks is guilty of disorderly conduct.

Laws for Kids

In Jupiter Inlet Colony, Florida, stubborn children are considered vagrants.

In the state of Washington, it's illegal to pretend that your parents are rich.

In Roderfield, West Virginia, only babies are allowed to ride in baby carriages.

If you live in the state of Louisiana, you can grow as tall as you want.

In Lynn, Massachusetts, babies may not be given coffee.

Lucky that Ringo, John, George, and Paul were from Liverpool because it's against the law in Mesquite, Texas, for youngsters to have unusual haircuts.

It's for the Birds

In California, it is against the law to detain a homing pigeon.

In Utah, birds have the right of way on public highways.

In Oklahoma, it is illegal to steal a bird's nest from a public cemetery.

It is illegal to sell or buy a buzzard in Ohio, because they are classified as "songbirds."

In Bayonne, New Jersey, it is against the law for a pigeon to fly overhead without a license.

It's for the Beasts

In Atlanta, it is against the law to secure a giraffe to a telephone pole or street lamp.

In Los Angeles, it is against the law to have a hippopotamus in your possession.

In Alaska, it is against the law to disturb a grizzly bear for the purpose of taking its picture.

In Galveston, Texas, it is against the law for camels to wander the streets unattended.

In Arkansas, it is illegal to blindfold cows on public highways.

In Norfolk, Virginia, it is against the law for hens to lay eggs before 8 A.M. or after 4 P.M.

Men in Fruithill, Kentucky, must remove their hats when they come face to face with a cow.

It's a Dog's Life

In Chicago, it is against the law to take a French poodle to the opera.

In Hartford, Connecticut, your dog cannot get an education.

In Pauling, Ohio, a police officer may bite a dog in an attempt to quiet him.

In Barber, North Carolina, it is illegal for cats and dogs to fight.

In International Falls, Minnesota, cats are forbidden to chase dogs up telephone poles.

People who make ugly faces at dogs in Oklahoma will be fined and/or jailed.

Horsin' Around

In Wilbur, Washington, it is against the law to ride down the street on an ugly horse.

In Marshalltown, Iowa, it is against the law for a horse to eat a fire hydrant.

In Fountain Inn, South Carolina, all horses are required to wear pants in public.

In New York City, you can go to jail if you open your umbrella in the presence of a horse.

If you're riding through Charleston, South Carolina, your horse better be wearing diapers.

In Waco, Texas, it's illegal to toss a banana peel on the streets, because a horse could step on the peel and slip.

Splish, Splash . . .

A Florida law requires you to wear clothing when taking a bath.

A law in Boston, Massachusetts, has rendered it against the law to bathe without a written prescription from a doctor.

Falling asleep in a bathtub in Detroit, Michigan, is illegal.

Everyone must take a bath on Saturday night in Barre, Vermont.

Taking a bath in the winter months is against the law in Indiana.

In Brooklyn, New York, it is illegal for a donkey to sleep in a bathtub.

The Big Apple

In New York, it's against the law to do anything that's against the law.

Brainteasers

To solve these tantalizing teasers, you'll need to think carefully and logically. No special knowledge is required, just common sense.

Meet a pair of twins—one of whom always lies while the other always tells the truth, and see if you can figure out which one you're talking to.

Solve a murder on a train, as four fellow passengers speak only two sentences each.

Figure out whether you should sint or sant and whether you need to wear clothes when you do it.

Use your imagination, stay alert, and keep an open mind, and you'll have a good shot at solving these tricky logic puzzles, lateral thinking puzzles, and brain bafflers. Try them on your friends!

1. Thirty-two students took a nationwide exam and all the students from New York passed it. If the students from New York made up exactly 5% of the total number of the students that passed the test, how many students passed it, and how many students were from New York?

2. In a singles tennis tournament, 111 players participated. They used a new ball for each match. When a player lost one match, he was eliminated from the tournament. How many balls did they need?

3. We have ten glasses sitting in a row. The first five are filled with water and the other five are empty. What are the minimum number of glasses needed to move so that the full and empty glasses alternate?

4. If two ducks are swimming in front of another duck, two ducks are swimming behind another duck, and one duck is swimming between two other ducks, what is the minimum number of ducks?

5. A little bird weighing 5 ounces (140 g) is sleeping in a cage. We put the cage on a scale and it weighs one pound (454 g). The bird then wakes up and starts flying all over the cage. What will the scale indicate while the bird is in the air?

6. If yesterday was Wednesday's tomorrow, and tomorrow is Sunday's yesterday, what day is today?

7. We have just invented two words: to "sint" and to "sant." You cannot sint or sant in the street or in the principal's office. You can do both things in the bathroom, the school's swimming pool, and at the public beach, but in the swimming pool and the beach you had better not sint completely. You cannot sint without clothes on, and you need little or no clothing to sant. Can you guess what these words mean?

8. "This parrot can repeat anything it hears," the owner of the pet shop told Rick last week. So he bought it. Yesterday he went to return it, claiming that the parrot had not said even one word. However, the pet shop owner had not lied to him. Can you explain this?

9. Peter and Paul are twin brothers. One of them (we don't know which) always lies. The other one always tells the truth. I ask one of them:

"Is Paul the one that lies?"
"Yes," he answers.
Did I speak to Peter or Paul?

10. This morning I had to take the stairs because the elevator was out of service. I had already gone down seven steps when I saw Professor Zizoloziz on the ground floor coming up. I continued descending at my usual pace, greeted the professor when we passed, and was surprised to see that when I still had four more steps to go, the professor had gone up the whole flight. "When I go down one step, he goes up two," I thought. How many steps does the staircase have?

1 1. After heaven, earth, the grass, and all the animals were created, the snake, who was very smart, decided to make its own contribution. It decided to lie every Tuesday, Thursday, and Saturday. For the other days of the week, it told the truth.

"Hey, Eve, honey, why don't you try an apple?" the snake suggested.

"But I'm not allowed to," said Eve.

"Oh, no," said the snake. "You can eat it today since it's Saturday and God is resting."

"No, not today," said Eve. "Maybe tomorrow."

"Tomorrow is Wednesday and it will be too late," insisted the snake.

This is how the snake tricked Eve.

What day of the week did this conversation take place?

1 2. Here is a puzzle from Lewis Carroll's book of puzzles, riddles, and anagrams, *A Tangled Tale*, written in 1885.

The governor wanted to give a small dinner, and so he invited only the following guests: his father's brother-in-law; his brother's father-in-law, his father-in-law's brother, and his brother-in-law's father. How many guests came to dinner?

1 3. The midnight train is coming down the mountain. Arthur Farnanski seems to be dozing in his seat. Someone knows this is not true.

At the station, all the passengers get off of the train, except one. The conductor comes and taps him on the shoulder to let him know they have arrived. Arthur Farnanski does not answer. He is dead.

"His heart?" asks the conductor, looking at the dead body.

"Strychnine," answers the forensics doctor.

Hours later, the four people who had shared the train compartment with the dead man are at the police station.

The man in the dark suit said, "I'm innocent. The blonde woman was talking to Farnanski."

The blonde woman said, "I'm innocent. I did not speak to Farnanski."

The man in the light suit said, "I'm innocent. The brunette woman killed him."

The brunette woman said, "I'm innocent. One of the men killed him."

That same morning while serving coffee, the waiter at the diner asks the inspector, "This is an easy case for you, isn't it?"

"Yes," answers the inspector. "Four true statements and four false ones. Easy as pie."

Who killed Farnanski? (Only one person is guilty.)

14. Suppose a low-calorie donut has 95 percent fewer calories than a regular donut. How many low-calorie donuts would you need to eat to take in as many calories as you'd get from a regular donut?

15. Puzzlemaker Lewis Carroll, author of *Alice in Wonderland*, invented this puzzle. Four men and their wives wanted to cross the river in a boat that could hold only two people at a time. The conditions were:

　a. A man could not leave his wife on the bank without him unless she was either alone or with one or more women.

　b. Someone had to bring the boat back.

How did they do it?

16. A portable waffle machine makes 120 waffles per minute. A stationary waffle machine makes three waffles per second. How many portable machines would you need if you wanted to equal the output of four stationary machines?

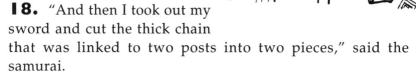

17. The ages of a father and a son add up to 55. The father's age is the son's age reversed. How old are they?

18. "And then I took out my sword and cut the thick chain that was linked to two posts into two pieces," said the samurai.

　"That is not true," said the monk.

How did the monk know the samurai's story was untrue?

19. Two investors—we'll call them Smith and Jones— made some unfortunate decisions in the stock market. Smith lost 60 percent of his money and Jones lost 85 percent. Jones was so discouraged, he took his money out and put it into a savings bank. Smith, on the other hand, made some additional investments in an effort to get his money back. But he wasn't any luckier the second time around—he lost another 60 percent.

Well, neither of them made a very strong showing, that much is certain. But who did worse, Smith or Jones?

20. John Cash saw his face on a poster nailed to a tree. As he approached, he saw:

WANTED—DEAD OR ALIVE

Under his picture, it read:

REWARD ____ DOLLARS

There was a 3-digit figure on the poster. John drew his Colt and shot at the first number (in the hundreds column).

He had just reduced the price on his head by 5 times.

"Good Lord!" said the doctor's daughter, who was sitting on the other side of the tree doing her math homework.

John blushed and shot again at another number (in the tens column).

He had just reduced the price on his head by another 5 times.

"Nice shooting!" said the young girl.

"Thank you, miss," said John. He spurred his horse and never returned.

What was the initial reward offered on John's head?

Knock 'em Dead

No matter how many knock-knocks you've heard, you'll find some new ones here to laugh at, groan at, and lob at your friends. This zany chapter features over 50 wacky knock-knocks that will keep you and your buddies in stitches for as long as you want to trade knock-knock jokes.

Find out what's happening when Adolf comes calling— or Amahl, or Darren, or Izzy. Get ready! The gang's all here, and they're knock-knocking at your door!

Knock-Knock.

Who's there?
Adolf.
Adolf who?
Adolf ball hit me in the mowf.

Knock-Knock.
Who's there?
Amahl.
Amahl who?
Amahl shook up.

Knock-Knock.
Who's there?
Amana.
Amana who?
Amana bad mood!

Knock-Knock.
  Who's there?
Darren.
  Darren who?
Darren young man on
  the flying trapeze.

Knock-Knock.
  Who's there?
Deduct.
  Deduct who?
Donald Deduct.

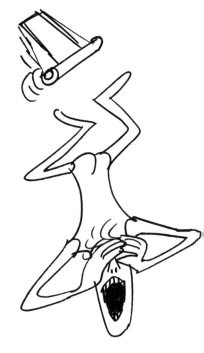

        Knock-Knock.
          Who's there?
        Dennis.
          Dennis who?
        Dennis anyone?

Knock-Knock.
  Who's there?
Daryl.
  Daryl who?
Daryl never ever be another you.

Knock-Knock.
Who's there?
Dimitri.
Dimitri who?
Dimitri is where the lamb chops grow.

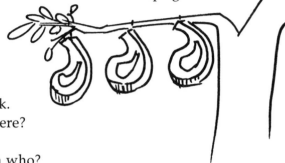

Knock-Knock.
Who's there?
Don Juan.
Don Juan who?
Don Juan to go to school today.

Knock-Knock.
Who's there?
Duane.
Duane who?
Duane the bathtub—I'm
dwowning.

Knock-Knock.
　　Who's there?
Gerald.
　　Gerald who?
Gerald washed up, kid.

Knock-Knock.
　　Who's there?
Gorilla.
　　Gorilla who?
Gorilla cheese sandwich.

　　　　Knock-Knock.
　　　　　　Who's there?
　　　　Hardy.
　　　　　　Hardy who?
　　　　Hardy-har-har!

Knock-Knock.
　　Who's there?
Hiawatha.
　　Hiawatha who?
Hiawatha very bad today.

Knock-Knock.
　Who's there?
Howell.
　Howell who?
Howell you have your pizza,
　plain or with sausage?

Knock-Knock.
　Who's there?
Hugo.
　Hugo who?
Hugo your way and I'll go mine.

Knock-Knock.
　Who's there?
Izzy.
　Izzy who?
Izzy come, Izzy go.

Knock-Knock.
　Who's there?
Ivan.
　Ivan who?
Ivan my mommy.

Knock-Knock.
   Who's there?
Jaws.
   Jaws who?
Jaws truly.

Knock-Knock.
   Who's there?
Jose.
   Jose who?
"Jose can you see, by the dawn's early light..."

Knock-Knock.
   Who's there?
Juan.
   Juan who?
Juan more time...

Knock-Knock.
   Who's there?
Jupiter.
   Jupiter who?
Jupiter fly in my soup?

Knock-Knock.
  Who's there?
Kenneth.
    Kenneth who?
Kenneth little kids play with you?

Knock-Knock.
  Who's there?
Leif.
    Leif who?
Leif me alone.

Knock-Knock.
  Who's there?
Luke.
    Luke who?
Luke before you leap.

Knock-Knock.
Who's there?
Llama.
Llama who?
"Llama Yankee Doodle Dandy..."

Knock-Knock.
Who's there?
Matthew.
Matthew who?
Matthew is pinthing my foot.

Knock-Knock.
Who's there?
Max.
Max who?
Max no difference. Open the door.

Knock-Knock.
Who's there?
Odysseus (pronounced Oh-diss-us).
Odysseus who?
Odysseus the last straw!

Knock-Knock.
Who's there?
Oliver.
Oliver who?
Oliver homework blew away.

Knock-Knock.
    Who's there?
Obadiah (pronounced O-bad-eye-ah).
    Obadiah who?
Obadiah from dis cold.

Knock-Knock.
    Who's there?
Orson.
    Orson who?
Orson around again?

Knock-Knock.
    Who's there?
Omar.
    Omar who?
Omar goodness—wrong door!

Knock-Knock.
    Who's there?
Oscar.
    Oscar who?
Oscar silly question, get a silly answer.

Knock-Knock.
    Who's there?
Otto.
    Otto who?
Otto tell the truth.

Knock-Knock.
> Who's there?

O'Shea.
> O'Shea who?

O'Shea, that's a shad shtory.

Knock-Knock.
> Who's there?

Plato.
> Plato who?

Plato spaghetti and
meatballs, please.

Knock-Knock.
> Who's there?

Robin.
> Robin who?

Robin the piggy bank again?

Knock-Knock.
> Who's there?

Roland.
> Roland who?

Roland stone gathers no moss.

Knock-Knock.
    Who's there?
Ping Pong.
    Ping Pong who?
Ping Pong, the witch is dead.

Knock-Knock.
    Who's there?
Rufus.
    Rufus who?
Rufus leaking and I'm getting wet.

Knock-Knock.
    Who's there?
Schachter.
    Schachter who?
Schachter Ripper.

Knock-Knock.
   Who's there?
Spider.
   Spider who?
Spider what everyone says, I like you.

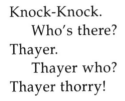

     Knock-Knock.
       Who's there?
     Thayer.
       Thayer who?
     Thayer thorry!

     Knock-Knock.
       Who's there?
     Tom Sawyer.
       Tom Sawyer who?
     Tom Sawyer underwear!

     Knock-Knock.
       Who's there?
     Arkansas.
       Arkansas who?
     Arkansas it too!

Knock-Knock.
   Who's there?
Toyota.
   Toyota who?
Toyota be a law against knock-knock jokes.

Knock-Knock.
   Who's there?
Twig.
   Twig who?
Twig or tweet!

Knock-Knock.
   Who's there?
Voodoo.
   Voodoo who?
Voodoo you think you are?

Knock-Knock.
   Who's there?
Who.
   Who who?
What are you—an owl?

Knock-Knock.
   Who's there?
Tad.
   Tad who?
Tad's all, folks!

Science Experiments

Shoot puffed rice pellets in all directions—without touching them! Turn a glass of water upside down without spilling any of it. Balance a paper clown on a thread! Create a hall of mirrors. The short, quick experiments in this chapter can be done just with ordinary things you've got around the house— and for some of them you don't need anything at all but your eyes and your fingers. Every one of them is amazing!

Water Bow

YOU NEED:
>   a plastic spoon
>   a woolen cloth

Rub a plastic spoon with a woolen cloth. Turn on a water tap gently and hold the spoon near the fine stream. The water will be pulled towards the spoon in a bow.

   The electric charge attracts the uncharged water particles. If the water touches the spoon, however, the effect is lost. Water conducts electricity and draws the charge into the spoon. Tiny water particles suspended in the air also take up electrical charge. Therefore, experiments with static electricity always work best on clear days and in centrally heated rooms.

Shooting Puffed Rice

YOU NEED:
- a plastic spoon
- a woolen cloth
- a dish containing puffed rice

Charge a plastic spoon with a woolen cloth and hold it over a dish containing puffed rice. The grains jump up and remain hanging on the spoon until suddenly they shoot wildly in all directions.

The puffed rice grains are attracted to the negatively charged spoon and cling to it for a time. Some of the electrons pass from the spoon into the puffed rice, until the grains and the spoon have the same charge. And because like charges repel one another, the puffed rice grains fly away from the spoon.

Hanging Water

YOU NEED:
> a glass filled with water
> a postcard

Do this one over a sink!

Fill a glass to overflowing with water and lay a postcard on it. Support the postcard with one hand and turn the glass upside down. Then remove your hand from the card. It remains on the glass, and allows no water to escape.

With a glass of normal height, a weight of water of about 2 ounces (57 g) presses down on each square inch of the card. At the same time, however, the pressure of air pushing upward on the postcard from below is about 100 times as great on each square inch. The air pressure holds the card so firmly against the glass that no air can enter at the side, and no water can flow out.

Strong Egg

YOU NEED:
> an egg
> a plastic bag
> 2 walnuts

Want to bet that you can crack walnuts more easily in your hand than a raw hen's egg?

Take a slightly polished egg and place your hand (as a precaution) in a plastic bag, and squeeze as hard as you can.

The pressure of your fingers is distributed evenly from all sides onto the egg and is not enough—if the shell is undamaged—to break it. Curved surfaces are extremely strong. People use this advantage in the building of arches and bridges, and cars hardly have a flat surface for the same reason. You can easily crack two walnuts, however, in one hand, because the pressure is concentrated at the points of contact.

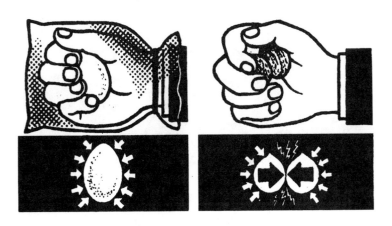

The Balancing Clown

YOU NEED:
>thick writing paper
>pencil
>clown drawing on this page
>glue
>2 small coins
>crayons or paint

Trace the large clown onto thick writing paper, cut out two figures, and glue both pieces together with two small coins placed in the hands, so that they are invisible. Color the figure brightly. The little paper clown will balance everywhere—on a pencil point, on your finger, or as a tightrope walker on a thread. This trick baffles everybody. It would seem that the figure should fall because its top half appears heavier.

To be traced

The weight of the coins causes the center of gravity of the figure to shift to under the nose, so that it remains balanced.

The Paper Bridge

YOU NEED:
> a sheet of writing paper
> 3 glasses

Lay a sheet of writing paper as a bridge across two glasses, and place a third glass on it. The bridge collapses. But if you fold the paper as shown, it supports the weight of the glass. Vertical surfaces are much less sensitive to pressure and stress than are those laid flat. The load of the tumbler is distributed over several sloping paper walls. They are supported in the folds and thus have a very high stability. In practice the stability is increased by molding sheets and slabs to give rounded or angled sections. Think about the strength of corrugated iron and corrugated cardboard.

Bottle Ghost

YOU NEED:
>   an empty bottle, cooled
>   water
>   a coin

An empty bottle that has been stored in a cool place has a ghost in it.

Moisten the rim of the bottle's mouth with water and cover it with a coin. Place your hands on the bottle. Suddenly the coin will move as if by a ghostly hand.

The cold air in the bottle is warmed by your hands and expands, but is prevented from escaping by the water between the bottle rim and the coin. However, when the pressure is great enough, the coin behaves like a valve, lifting up and allowing the warm air to escape.

Magic Spiral

YOU NEED:

  no special equipment

Look at this picture closely. You will probably be sure that you are seeing a spiral. But check it with a pair of compasses and you'll see that the picture is of concentric circles. The individual sections of the circles seem to be moving in a spiral toward the middle of the picture because of the special type of background.

The Disappearing Finger

YOU NEED:
  no special equipment

Cover your left eye with your right hand and look straight
ahead with your right eye. Raise your left forefinger to your
left ear and move it until the tip of the finger is just visible,
as in picture A.

  If you now move your eye to look directly at the finger
(as in picture B), strangely enough, your finger will disappear.

  This interesting experiment has a geometrical explanation:
when you are looking straight ahead (A), the light rays from
the finger pass over the bridge of your nose into the pupil of
your eye. But if your pupil is moved to the left (B), the light
rays from the finger go past it.

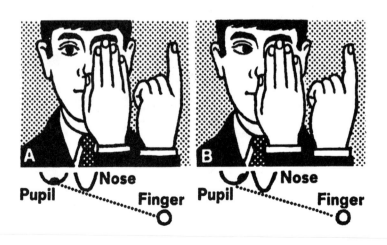

Humming Flute

YOU NEED:
>   a square piece of paper
>   scissors

Take a square piece of paper and snip one corner off. Then make two notches in the opposite corner. Roll the paper in the direction of the arrow in the picture to make a tube about as thick as a pencil, and fold the notched corner to cover the opening. Draw a deep breath through the tube. This creates a loud humming sound. The paper corner is sucked up by the air drawn in, but since it is slightly springy, it begins to vibrate. The vibration is quite slow, so it makes a deep sound.

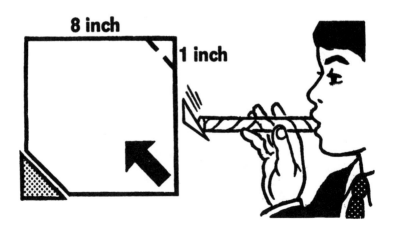

8 inch

1 inch

Unusual Magnification

YOU NEED:
> a card
> a needle
> a newspaper

Make a small hole in a card with a needle. Hold it close to your eye and look through it. If you bring a newspaper very close, you will see to your surprise that the type is much larger and clearer.

   This phenomenon is caused by the refraction of light. The light rays passing through the small hole are made to bend and spread out, and so the letters appear larger. The sharpness of the image is caused—as in a camera—by the shuttering effect of the small opening. The part of the light radiation that would make the image blurred is held back.

View into Infinity

YOU NEED:
>   a pocket mirror
>   a larger mirror

Hold a pocket mirror between your eyes so that you can look to both sides into a larger mirror. If you place the mirrors parallel to one another, you will see an infinite series of reflections, which stretches into the distance like a hall of mirrors.

Since the glass of the mirror shines with a slightly greenish tint, some light is absorbed at each reflection, so that the image becomes less sharp with increasing distance.

Magic Tricks

The magic tricks in this chapter will not only fool your friends, but are also interesting, surprising, and amusing. None of them requires any special dexterity or a lot of practice. You can perform most of them with everyday objects.

Pull strings through your neck or your friend's arm! Tie a knot in a rope and then pull it off. Prove that you have magic fingers. Perform feats of mental telepathy!

String Out

YOU NEED:

a length of string or cord about 4 feet (1.2 m) long.

Tie the ends in a square knot. Stick your thumbs inside the loop and extend the string. Display the string at about neck level for all to see.

Say, "Now here's a real riddle for you. Do I have a magic neck or a magic string? I'll let you decide."

Without removing your thumbs, swing the looped string over your head so that the string is behind your neck like this:

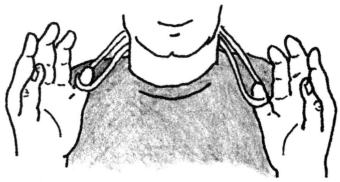

For clarity, the string in all of these drawings is shown to be thicker than it actually is.

"Now watch carefully."

Quickly bring your hands together and insert your left first (index) finger into the loop just behind your right thumb, and pull to the left with your index finger.

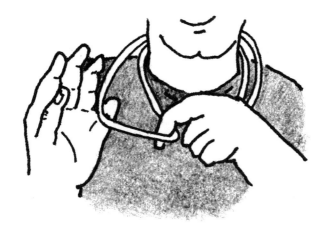

This shows the beginning of the movement.

Your left thumb naturally drops out of the loop, but only momentarily. Immediately, and without halting the motion, place your left thumb next to your left index finger and let the thumb take over the pulling motion to the left. Your left index finger will automatically be disengaged from the loop.

Snap your thumbs against the inside of the loop as you extend the string forward. The position now is the same as at the beginning. Apparently, you've pulled the string through your neck!

The entire movement is done in a fraction of a second. After you've practiced it a half dozen times, you'll have mastered it for life.

VARIATIONS

You can do this trick in other ways. For example, pull the string through a belt loop. Most effective is to place the string around a spectator's arm and then, apparently, pull it right through the arm.

String Out II

YOU NEED:

    a looped string

Using the same looped string from the previous trick, you can perform another escape.

    Hold the string between your two hands, fingers pointed towards yourself, like this:

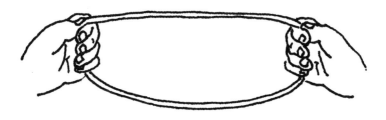

    Bring the right side of the string over the left side, forming a small loop inside the larger loop.

    Between your teeth, lightly hold the portion where the strings cross.

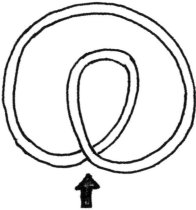

Grip with teeth here.

Stick your left thumb into the end of the larger loop, pulling it fairly tight, so that the smaller loop will be below it. Now, from below, stick your right index finger up through the smaller loop. Bring that finger over the right side of the larger loop under the left side, and to your nose. The dark arrow below shows the route of your index finger to your nose.

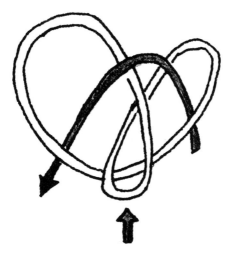

Continue holding your right index finger to the tip of your nose as you pull the larger loop with your left thumb and release the string from your teeth. The string comes free, apparently passing right through your finger.

The Sliding Knot

Have you ever seen this trick? The magician cuts a length of rope into two pieces and ties two of the ends together. A spectator holds the loose ends. The magician grasps the knot in the middle and slides it right off the rope, and the rope is completely restored.

The effect is amazing. Here's a version you can do.

YOU NEED:

a length of string or cord 3 feet (1 m) in length
scissors

Tie the ends of the cord together, forming a loop. Hold this loop between your hands, fingers pointed towards you, like this:

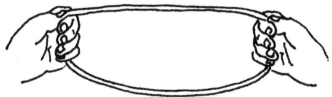

Now rotate your left hand, turning the string and forming a double loop. This is what spectators will assume you're doing, if you are sneaky. When you form that double loop, you give the string an extra half-turn with your left hand. So, when you stretch out the double loop, a portion of the string is interlocked, as shown below:

Naturally, you don't want spectators to see this interlocked portion. So as you double the loop, quickly slide your right hand along the doubled string and conceal the interlock.

Move your left hand to within a few inches (10 cm) of your right, so that you're offering a small length of string for a helpful spectator—let's call him Craig—to cut with the scissors. This is how to offer it.

You very wisely hand Craig the scissors before you start playing with the string. Invariably, your helper will cut at about the middle of the portion you offer him.

Double loop concealed here.

Hold up the string in your right hand, demonstrating that it's in two pieces. Making sure you keep the interlock concealed with your right fingers, carefully tie the ends of the small piece into a square knot. Now you no longer need to conceal anything.

Ask Craig to hold the two loose ends of the string. Make some mystical waves over the string, mumbling some magic words. Look a little disappointed. Try again. You're even more disappointed.

"The magic doesn't seem to be working," you tell Craig. "But I'd like to give you a little something for helping out. I know you won't take money, so what can I give you? I've got it!"

Slide the knot along the string, moving his hand to one side as you remove the knot from the string. Present him with the knot. Hold up the string by the ends.

"Say! That is a sort of magic."

The Disjointed Digit

YOU NEED:
> no special equipment

This trick works particularly well for children, but most adults are also amused by it. Apparently, you remove the index finger of your right hand.

"I have some amazing feats for you. Actually, they're not feats, but hands. Just watch these magic fingers."

Wiggle your fingers, demonstrating their amazing flexibility. Position your left hand so that your fingers point down and the back of your hand is toward the spectators. Tuck your left thumb into your left palm. Bring your left hand in front of your right. Bend in the index finger of your right hand. Your left hand, of course, conceals this. Rest your left hand on the back of your right hand, like this.

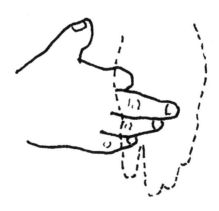

Twist your left hand upward, raising your second, third, and fourth fingers. Your index finger stays down, hiding the fact that your left thumb is bent inward. The illusion is that your left thumb is the outer joint of your right index finger.

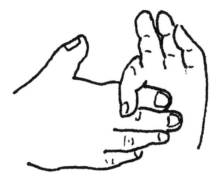

Move your thumb along the surface of your right second finger several times, demonstrating that the outer joint of your right index finger is separated from the rest of your finger, like this:

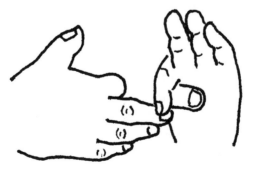

Then extend your left fingers again and straighten out your right index finger, grasping it in your left hand. Twist your right hand several times in a semicircle, "repairing" your finger. Hold up your right index finger and waggle it, showing that it's fully restored.

The Incredible Shrinking Finger

YOU NEED:
> no special equipment

Not only can you remove one of your fingers, but you can also shrink one.

Hold up your left hand straight, the back of your hand to onlookers. Grip the little finger of your left hand with your right hand. The index finger and thumb of your right hand hold the top knuckle. The remaining fingers of your right hand are cupped outward, like this:

Push downward with your right thumb and index finger, holding the top of your finger straight. At the same time, however, bend the lower knuckle of your little finger outward. You're concealing this bend with your second, third, and fourth right fingers.

Very slowly, push your little finger down, laboriously reducing its size. The illusion is quite realistic, since the tip of your finger remains pointing upward, and the finger slides down next to straight, extended fingers.

Agonize as you pull your finger back up. Repeat the reduction. You might even try a third time. Finally pull your finger back up, grasp it with your right hand, and rub the finger vigorously. Then show your left hand, moving all the fingers to show that everything is as it should be.

Give 'em the Slip

YOU NEED:
> a sheet of paper or a napkin
> pen or pencil

This is either magic at its finest, or the silliest trick of all time. Some people will think you're a fabulous magician.

You'll need eight little pieces of paper, so tear up a napkin or a sheet of paper.

Take a pen or a pencil, and, holding one of the pieces of paper, in the palm of your hand (so that no one can see it), say, "Will someone please give me a first name?"

You write down the name on the piece of paper, fold the paper, and toss it onto the table.

Take another piece of paper, ask for a name, write it on the paper, fold it, and toss it too, on the table. Repeat this procedure for all eight pieces of paper. Mix up the slips.

"While I turn my head, I'd like you to pick out any one of the pieces." Someone—let's say Suzy—does that.

"Open it up and look at the name." Suzy looks.

With your head still turned away, you say, "The name is Dennis." And sure enough, you're right.

"A simple case of mental telepathy," you explain.

Wait a few minutes, gather up the other papers, and discard them. If no one objects, you've performed a superb piece of magic. But if the spectators open up some of the other papers, they will discover that the same name is written on each one—because you wrote the first name given on every slip!

In the first instance (if you discard the slips), it will seem that you've performed a miracle. Otherwise, you've presented a comical stunt.

Coin Con

YOU NEED:
   a coin

No skill is required for this effective little fooler, but the timing must be perfect.

Show a coin in the palm of your right hand—any size coin will do. Bounce the coin of your hand a few times so that it moves toward your fingers. With your right thumb, move the coin to your fingertips where you grip it between thumb and fingers, like this:

Note that the coin is protruding a bit beyond the fingers. Hold your right hand up, its back toward the spectators.

Turn your left hand palm down and make it into a fist. Tell the spectators, "With this coin and this fist, I'm going to attempt a feat that some of the greatest magicians in the world are incapable of—I'm going to pass a solid through a solid."

With your right hand, push the coin against the back of your left hand. It should look like this to the spectators:

Withdraw your right hand, still holding the coin, which should be out of sight.

Turn your left hand over and open it. "There you are. The

coin has passed right through..."

You look puzzled. Look at your left hand in disbelief. Show the coin in your right hand. Toss it onto the open palm of your left hand. Extend your left hand so that the spectators can see the coin there.

"That's what you were supposed to see when I opened my hand."

Shake your head. "Some of the world's greatest magicians can't do it. I guess that makes me one of the world's greatest magicians."

As you say this, pick up the coin with your right hand. Turn your left hand palm down and make it into a fist. "I'll try one more time."

Push the coin against the back of your left hand. Withdraw your right hand. Turn your left hand over and open it, showing the coin lying in your palm.

You have passed a solid through a solid!

Oh, a detail got left out! You don't actually pick up the coin with your right hand. You leave it in the palm of your left hand. Tilt your left hand back toward you slightly while starting to reach toward the left palm, like this:

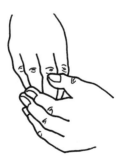

The spectators will see only the back of your two hands. Your right fingers and thumb are separated by about two inches as you reach.

Your right hand dips into the left. Your fingers are in front of the coin and the thumb is behind it. The right fingers scrape across the palm toward your right thumb, which remains motionless. This movement of your right fingers is what creates the illusion that you are picking up the coin.

As your right hand starts to withdraw, your left hand forms a fist, like this:

Your hands move apart. Your left hand, now a fist, turns palm down. Your right hand is held up, apparently displaying the coin. The drawing at right shows your view:

This display is quite brief. It's at this point that you say, "I'll try one more time."

You now duplicate the action you performed as you tried to push the coin through the back of your hand. Withdraw your right hand. For all the spectators know, the coin could still be in your right hand. So, to properly flummox everybody, don't show the right hand immediately.

Instead, say, "Let's see if it worked this time."

Turn your left hand over, open it, and show the coin. Only then, open your right hand, and show that it's empty. Smile, and say "Good!"

Secret Hiding Places

Where do you keep your letters and notes? Your valuables? And all the things you never want to lose?

You can keep your favorite items safe without a safe or even a lock. Open your eyes to boring little places where nobody looks. Build fake walls and other secret vaults. Leave innocent, stray clues that guide your friends to your special coded maps, and more.

You'll discover secret hiding places at home, at school, and in between. Just don't forget where you hid this book. Now hide it!

The Trapdoor Box

YOU NEED:
>   2 similar shoe boxes or a plain cardboard box
>   newspaper
>   scissors
>   pencil
>   tape
>   butter knife

Here's a simple, deceptive vault that's easy to make and easy to ignore. It hides paper, comics, cards, and other flat items up to 1 inch (2.5 cm) high.

MAKING IT

1. Pick a cardboard box or shoe box that looks plain and boring.

2. Get a second box of the same color and material. One side of this box will be cut up to make the false bottom of the vault box. Make sure it's big enough and doesn't have holes.

3. Measure the bottom of the vault box with some newspaper. Spread it out and crease the paper's edges to make an accurate impression.

4. Cut the paper along the creased edges with scissors. Take a pencil and trace the paper along the second box. You're measuring the exact sides of your false bottom.

5. On the second box, cut out the cardboard carefully. Make sure one side has no writing on it.

HIDING IT

1. Lay your treasure flat. Comics, cards, etc., should be in tight plastic bags. Tape down each bag to make sure nothing will slide around. Help the new bottom sit evenly—fold up extra cardboard to fill in big gaps. Don't hide so much that the bottom looks fake!

2. Keeping your hands at the edges, push in the false bottom. Don't rush it, since air has to come out. When the false bottom lies flat, fill it with things that won't crush your treasure. Then, leave your vault in a corner or a closet. Put stuff on and around it and make it look ignored.

OPENING IT

Remove the stuff on top of the vault. Turn the box over. The bottom should slide down. If it's tight, take a butter knife and gently pry out the edges of the false bottom. Make sure you don't pull too hard and dent the false bottom. Don't give away clues!

The Hollow Book

Here's a long-term hiding place that's worth reading about. And it will cover your stuff perfectly. It hides anything that's the size of a cassette tape box, or smaller.

YOU NEED:
  a big, unwanted
    hardcover book
  cardboard
  pencil
  scissors
  ballpoint pen
  tape

MAKING IT

Note: This project needs an adult's permission and help with the cutting.

1. Select a book. Don't wreck a book that someone might want to read. Go to a used bookstore and find a big, cheap, old hardcover book. Or ask for a damaged book you can have for free. Pick a boring book that won't attract readers. Suggested titles: *1953 Travel Guide to Bolivia, You Can Be a Blacksmith, Why I Yodel,* and *Introducing Television: It's Radio with Pictures.* Or use an old phone book.

2. You want a sturdy book, so don't cut too big a hole.

First, you need to make a pattern. Cut a rectangular piece of cardboard that leaves a few inches on each side.

If the book is big enough, use a videotape box as a guide. If your book is smaller, use a cassette tape box.

3. Leave several pages at the beginning of the book to hide your hole. Then fit the rectangular pattern on the page where your hole begins. Leave at least an inch on each side. Use a pencil to trace the pattern.

4. Now ask an adult to poke one sharp point of the scissors into a corner of the outline. Once the scissors go through the page, cut the center out normally.

5. Take a ballpoint pen and trace the cutout page on the one beneath it. Repeat this on each page until you're most of the way through the book. Be sure to leave several pages uncut at the end for extra support.

HIDING IT

You may want to tape the inside pages of your book together so that nothing falls out. That's okay, but put the tape inside the hole only, along the cutout edges, like making walls or a swimming pool. Don't stick tape between the pages. You can see it from the outside, and it will become a bookmark that opens right to the secret hole. Not so secret!

Whatever you hide should sit right in the hole, and not bulge. If you used a tape box for a pattern, try tucking the box inside the book for extra protection. Then put your secret book up on a shelf next to other books you don't read often.

The Empty Boom Box

This vault may take a bit more work, but it's worth the effort and fools basically everybody. Get permission, and don't break anything that still works. It will hide whatever will fit inside!

YOU NEED:
> boom box, broken
> screwdriver
> scissors or wire cutters
> masking tape

MAKING IT

1. Make sure the boom box you're going to use is already broken. If you don't have an old one, go to an electronics repair shop and ask if they have a broken one you can have. If they won't give one away, maybe you can buy one for a small amount. These instructions work for a broken VCR as well.

2. Disconnect the electrical cord and throw it away. You do not want to even think about electricity near your vault.

3. With a screwdriver, remove the screws that hold the case together. Put these screws in a special place for safekeeping. Pull the two halves apart. Don't remove the screws on the handle unless it's the only way to open the case.

4. Almost every boom box is made the same way—the insides are really one piece. These guts stay in place with just a few screws, so all the machinery pulls out easily. Finding the screws isn't hard. They're usually at the edges, and sometimes in the middle of the case. Unscrew any screws you want, then give the entire inside a pull. Eventually it will budge!

Speaker wires may need to be cut with scissors or wire cutters. Though you can pull out parts without fear (and with fun), be careful of the cassette tape door—you don't want it to fall off!

HIDING IT

Once the case is hollow you can cover any inside edges with masking tape, if they seem sharp. Fit your secret treasures inside any way you want. If you wrap them, they won't rattle when they move. Put the cover back on and use the screws you put aside. Move your vault somewhere you would usually put a broken boom box, like a closet floor or under the bed—and forget about it!

The Lumpy Pillow

You can rest assured you'll always be comfortable using this secret vault. It hides solid objects of any size, depending on your pillow.

YOU NEED:
old foam couch
    cushion
sock, washcloth, or
    little towel
tape

MAKING IT
It all begins by choosing a stiff but spongy pillow, the kind most people have on a couch—not a bed pillow. Does yours match these critical requirements?

• It's filled only with foam—no feathers!
• It's got a zipper for easy access.
• It's not incredibly ugly or smelly, so nobody will throw it away one day.
• It's not incredibly nice, so nobody will care if you use it. Get permission.
• It's not incredibly expensive, worth no more than a small amount.

Open the zipper and take out the piece of foam. You may have to scrunch it in the middle to get it out.

Look at your foam. You're going to hollow out the middle, then cover the whole with some of the foam. Use your hands to pluck out little pieces of foam. Don't pull out too much foam, or the pillow won't fool anyone.

Stop plucking when your hole is a good size and there's still enough foam around the edges to feel like a normal pillow.

HIDING IT
Put your treasures inside the pillow, maybe wrapped in a sock, washcloth, or little towel to keep it soft. Make sure there's room to put some of the foam back on top.

Choose a few foam pieces you took out. Tape them together from the inside to make a plug for the top of the hole. You want to feel foam on the outside—not tape. Put in the plug.

Put your pillow back into its case. Zip the zipper and toss it casually on the bed, or put it in a corner, or stick it in the closet. You don't want other people sleeping on it. As with any pillow, use your head.

The Video Vault

This little vault is a real star—it's compact, it's fast, and it's supereasy to ignore. It hides anything that fits inside a videotape box—about the size of a small paperback book.

YOU NEED:

a jammed or broken videotape
a small screwdriver
black electrical tape or
    construction paper

MAKING IT

Pick a jammed or broken videotape. Or pick a bad video that's worth the sacrifice. If it's not yours, get permission. And make sure it's the kind of videotape that's held together with screws.

Open the plastic case with a little screwdriver and save the screws. Then turn the case over.

Remove the cover. See the little piece of plastic that covers the tape? Look for a square button in the corner to push. Push it. Now you can get to the tape. Take out all the contents.

Take some black construction paper or black electrical tape. Put it on the inside of the clear plastic window (if there is one) to hide your stuff from view. Or if you have a sticker that can cover the window from the outside, write the name of your "movie" on it.

HIDING IT

Tuck your treasures inside the black tape box. Tape it down or use stuffing so that nothing shakes around. Try not to make it too heavy or it'll feel fake. Put the screws back in. Then put it back into its printed box and bury it on the boring end of your video pile. Don't make it a good movie! Make up dumb movie titles like *Windmills of Miniature Golf*, *The Hog Farmer*, or *Stronger Elbows in 30 Days*. You could even write "broken" on it somewhere. Definitely don't put this in your VCR, or that's what will be broken.

The Secret Wall

This is one of the harder vaults to discover, because it's not simple to open. Use it for things you won't need often. It's great for hiding books, papers, comics, cards, and items up to a few inches thick.

YOU NEED:

a closet with shelves, low kitchen cupboard, or shelves behind a door
a piece of cardboard or Foamcore
a piece of plywood
newspaper
scissors
pencil
covering (cloth, paper, etc.)
4 empty thread spools, or empty plastic film canisters, about an inch (2.5 cm) deep
glue or tape
a piece of fish line or string about 6 inches (15 cm) longer than the wall

MAKING IT

1. Find a closet with built-in shelves, a low kitchen cupboard, or shelves behind a door. Pick a low shelf, if you can, because people are less likely to see the wall behind it when they're standing up.

2. Get material to use for your back wall. You can cut a piece of cardboard from a large box. You can use a light, stiff material called Foamcore, which is sold in art stores. You can work with an adult to cut a piece of plywood to fit your space. Or find another flat material that's bigger than the wall you're hiding, and that you can cut.

3. Measure the four sides of the back wall with some newspaper. Spread it out and crease the paper's edges along each side. Pull out the newspaper and cut it along the creased edges with scissors.

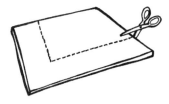

4. Place the newspaper on your wall material. Trace around the edges with a pencil to measure the wall.

5. If you can't safely cut your fake wall with scissors, ask an adult to help you.

6. Make sure your wall is the right color. Use paint, or cover it with paper, or stretch cloth across it so it isn't noticeable. Contact paper (sticky shelf paper) comes in lots of colors and even in wood-grain patterns.

7. Take four empty thread spools, or empty plastic film canisters, or something else about an inch deep. Glue them just inside each of the four corners of your fake wall, but not all the way to the corners.

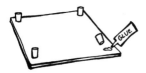

8. Cut a piece of fish line or string that's about 6 inches (15 cm) longer than the bottom of your wall. Tie small loops at each end; you'll pull these to open the wall. Glue or tape the line near the inside bottom edge, so that you can easily pull out your wall once it's in place. You can also run it toward the top, if that's more hidden.

HIDING IT

Stand your treasure up against the back wall. Think about using an envelope or bag to hold it in place; maybe even attach it to the real wall. Put your fake wall gently in place—making sure the loops are on the outside. Then put extra stuff in front to hide it.

OPENING IT

Just pull both secret string loops at the same time. Once the wall starts to come away, you can just use your hands.

Action Games Inside and Out

You don't have to go outdoors to play football, soccer, or other games that you never thought you could play in the house. This chapter shows how you can take part in fast action games whether you're indoors or out, with the help of some Velcro and tube socks. You can play a fast game of Target Ball, or go bowling in the hallway, and you won't get any objections from the adults in the house, either.

If the weather allows for outdoor action, there are some great ideas here too. Chalk up a square for Box Ball, which is played a little like tennis— or put a new twist on an old tradition and play stickball with a special kind of stick—a broom! Or put two great games together for a few rounds of Frisbee Golf.

Let the games begin!

Velcro Target Ball

Now you can finally throw things in the house!

YOU NEED:

> a medium-sized roll of self-sticking Velcro
> large piece of cardboard
> 2 ping-pong balls
> magic marker
> notepad and pencil

MAKING THE TARGET

Draw 4 to 6 concentric circles on a large piece of cardboard or poster board. The center circle is the bull's-eye and should be about the size of a piece of salami.

Decide how many points each circle should earn. Using the magic marker, write the smallest number in the largest circle. Write the next smallest number in the next largest, and so on, until you get to the smallest one. The bull's-eye is the hardest one to hit so it should be worth the most points.

Cut lots of pieces of Velcro about 1 inch (2.5 cm) long from one side of the roll of Velcro, and space them evenly within each circle, sticking on as many as you like. The larger the spaces between the pieces, the harder the game will be, because the balls will have fewer pieces of Velcro on which to stick.

Mount the target on a wall with tape.

MAKING THE BALLS

Using the leftover side of Velcro, cut out four strips about 4 inches (10 cm) long. They should be as wide as the Velcro roll.

Wrap one of the strips tightly around a ping-pong ball, sticking the ends of the Velcro together. Wrap another strip diagonally to cover the rest of the ball, and stick the ends together.

Do the same with the other ping-pong ball.

Stand about 10 feet (3 m) away and try to hit the Velcro pieces in the target circles with the ping-pong balls. A direct hit should cause the ball to stick to the target. Each player gets to throw both balls on each turn.

When a ping-pong ball sticks to the target, the player should write down the number of points earned on a scoreboard.

Add up a player's score at the end of each turn. The first player to get 150 points wins.

Hallway Bowling

Want to take bowling up to the next level and down your own hallway? In this game, pinball meets miniature golf. Just set 'em up and knock 'em down.

YOU NEED:
> 3–10 plastic water or soda bottles
> 3 balls (any small bouncy type)
> shoes, pillows, phone books, and other bumpers
> cardboard (from a cereal box or writing tablet)
> blanket

Set up your bowling alley. Get 3 to 10 clean plastic bottles. They're your pins. At one end of the hallway, set up the pins in a triangle. Make sure that the pins are close enough together so that when the first one falls over, it will knock the others down, too.

For the bowling balls, use tennis balls, squash balls, or any mix of similar bouncy balls.

At the very end of the hall, lay out the blanket to keep your bowling balls from rolling too far away.

Each bowler gets 3 turns. When you've used up all 3 balls, count how many pins you've knocked over. Then set them up for the next player.

Start simply. Try bowling straight down the lane a few times until you get the hang of knocking the pins down. Then try bouncing the ball off the walls so it ricochets off the sides of the alley.

After everyone has had a turn, you can rebuild the alley. Try adding a few obstacles—shoes, cushions, books, and so forth—to the hallway. Now you have to make your ball bounce around them on its way to the pins.

You can also build ramps to get the ball up and over some of the obstacles. Just prop up a piece of cardboard on a phone book or a shoe, and you're ready to fly.

VARIATION
You don't need a hard floor to bowl on. Bowling also works on a rug. Use a pair of rolled-up tube socks for the ball. Be sure to roll the ball. It's not as easy as it seems!

Tabletop Football

When you can't play football outside, it's time to play Tabletop Football. Using only one piece of paper, you and a friend can score touchdowns, field goals, and extra points all day without even leaving the table.

YOU NEED:
>a smooth table
>sheet of notebook paper
>scissors
>tape

MAKING THE FOOTBALL
These illustrations show the seven easy steps to making a football, using paper, scissors, and tape.

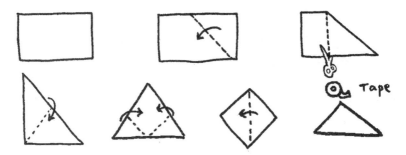

PLAYING THE GAME
The two football players sit on opposite sides of the table. The object is to flick the football across the table with your thumb and forefinger. You get three flicks to get the football hanging over the other player's end of the table without falling off.

SCORING

If you manage to get the football to hang off the other player's end of the table without falling off, you have scored a touchdown, which is worth 6 points.

If you score a touchdown, you get to try for one extra point.

If you knock the football off the table, the other player gets to try for a field goal, which is worth 3 points.

The first player to get 35 points wins.

FIELD GOALS AND EXTRA POINTS

The player who is not kicking: Make two Ls with your thumbs and index fingers. Then touch the thumbs together so that you get 3 sides of a square. Rest your wrists on the table (elbows make it harder). This forms what is called the "uprights."

The player who is kicking: To kick field goals and get extra points, hold the football between the table and your index finger. Using your other hand, flick the football using your thumb and middle finger. Try to kick it through the uprights. If it goes through, you get 3 points for a field goal or 1 point for an extra point.

Sock Soccer

Even if it's raining outside, you can still play soccer. You don't need a field, a ball, a goal, or a minivan to transport the team. Get yourself an extra pair of socks and make enough room to kick, pass, and score without getting a furniture-shaped dent in your head! Four or more can play.

YOU NEED:
> a pair of tube socks
> a towel
> clock or watch

To make your ball, take a pair of tube socks and roll them up inside each other. Make it as round as you can.

Mark off the playing field—as big an area as you'd need for a dance. On one end of the field, lay a towel on the floor, a couple of feet away from the wall. That's the goal. To score, you have to kick the ball so that it stays on the towel. If it rolls off or goes past the towel altogether, it's no good.

The wall at the other end of the room is the midfield. When the team that is defending the goal kicks the ball back to the midfield wall, it can try to score a goal.

Don't get too close! If the attacking players get so near the goal that they can step on it, they have to give up the ball to the other team. If any of the defenders get close enough to a shooter for the shooter to touch him, the shooter gets a free kick at the goal with no blocking allowed. (It's not fair for the shooter to chase the defender just to get a free shot.)

No fair using your hands to touch the ball. If a shooter touches it, it's the other team's turn to be on the offensive. If a defender does, the shooter gets a free shot at the goal.

At the end of 5 minutes, if no one has scored or kicked the ball back to the midfield, switch sides.

VARIATION

Use a human goalie. Assign one person to be the goalkeeper, who sits on the ground behind the goal. The goalie can touch the ball with his hands, head, or any other part of his body to keep it off the towel.

Box Ball

Box ball is not a ball shaped like a box. It's not a box shaped like a ball, either. But it's more fun. You need four or more for this game.

YOU NEED:
> chalk
> a soccer ball

Find a piece of pavement in a playground or schoolyard or other asphalt for your game. Draw a chalk square that's 8 feet (2.4 m) on each side. Then divide it into 4 small squares that measure 4 feet (1.2 m) on a side. Label the squares 1, 2, 3, and 4, counting clockwise.

Box Ball (also known as "Four Squares") is played a little like tennis. Each player stands inside one of the small squares. If there are more than four players, the extras should line up outside Square 4. The player in Square 1 serves by bouncing the ball in the square and then bonking it into one of the other squares. The player in that square then has to keep the ball in play by smacking it into any other square.

Hit the ball with an open hand or fist. No fair catching the ball and then throwing it back, or cradling the ball to get better control. That's called a "carry," and in cowboy days it would get you shot.

If the ball lands in your square and you don't hit it back, or if you hit the ball and it doesn't land in someone else's square, you're out. You're also out if you get hit with the ball, and it doesn't bounce off you into another square. Naturally, you're also out if someone calls you for a carry. But no shooting.

If there are only 4 players, the one who is out moves to Square 4 and everyone else moves "up a number" toward Square 1. If there are 5 or more players, the player who is out goes to the back of the line and the first person in line moves into Square 4.

HOT TIPS:
If you have fewer than 4 players, try playing "Two Squares." Just use half the court.

Decide if you want to allow "spinners." That's when you hit the ball on its side and make it spin so it bounces funnily when it hits the ground.

Batter-Up Broom Ball

In the 1950s, players from the New York Yankees used to play an inning or two in neighborhood stickball matches, using any stick they could find. Give a new function to the household sweeping tool—grab a broom and head out for a game of Broom Ball. Two or more can play.

YOU NEED:
>   chalk
>   ball (a racquetball, tennis ball, or squash ball is good)
>   bat (a broomstick, mop handle, or anything you can swing)

Pick a playing area. With just a few players, you can use a stoop or a wall, with the wall "playing" as catcher. With more players, you can play on pavement in a schoolyard or playground.

Safety note: Don't play in the street at all, or on a sidewalk that is close to a street where there is traffic.

Decide on the boundaries and the bases. Mark the distance a ball needs to be hit to count as a single, a double, a triple, or a home run. Use natural features for bases, like lampposts, tree stumps, or park benches, or mark them on the ground with chalk. If you're playing against a wall, draw a box for the strike zone on the wall. (It should be between the shoulders and the knees of most of the kids, and about 18 inches [45 cm] wide. And nowhere near windows.)

Choose teams and decide who gets to pitch first. The pitcher throws the ball toward the batter. It has to bounce once before it passes the batter.

Try to hit the pitch as far as you can. If you get a hit, check how far it went to see what kind of hit it was. If there is a player "on second base" and the next batter hits a double, the first player scores, because he gets to advance 2 bases, and that's home plate. A single plus a triple equals one run and one player on third, and so on.

If you swing and miss, hit a foul ball, or let the ball hit the strike zone, it is a strike. Three strikes and you're out. If you hit the ball and the other team catches it, you're out. When the hitting team gets 3 outs, it's their turn to pitch.

Decide how long you want to play and make sure each team gets a fair chance to bat before the game ends.

Change the rules to fit your neighborhood. You can run bases, just like regular baseball, if you have a good "field" to play on. If you're short on players, batters can "pitch" to themselves. Part of the fun of Broom Ball is making the rules fit your game.

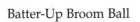

Frisbee Golf

Put a new spin on two old sports. It's not your grandfather's golf and it's not your big brother's Frisbee game. This combo is twice as much fun. One or more can play.

YOU NEED:

      1 Frisbee per person

      pencil and paper

Find a place to play with plenty of space.

    The idea is to throw your Frisbee so it hits a goal. Pick some targets with enough space around them for throwing. You can design a whole course ahead of time or decide the next goal as you play. (Traditional golf courses have 18 holes, but you can make as many as you want.)

    Take turns throwing your Frisbee toward the goal. Everyone should stand in the same spot to start.

    Once each player has thrown, walk together in the direction of the goal. As you reach each Frisbee, its owner gets to throw it again.

    Use the pencil and paper to keep track of how many throws it takes each person to hit the goal. To figure the final scores, add the totals for all the goals together. Lowest score wins.

	Carol	Mac	Jen
Big Tree	1	3	2
Bench	1	2	1
Little Tree	1	2	2
Trashcan	1	3	1
Total	4	10	6

Cartooning

Everyone likes to draw cartoons, but some people think they have to be trained artists to draw them. That's just not true. Anyone can draw great cartoons. The important thing to remember is that cartoonists have to think funny. In fact, being able to think funny is even more important for a cartoonist than being able to draw well. That's because cartoons have their origin in humor rather than art.

Here are lots of step-by-step ideas for drawing cartoon animals. As you draw along, remember that you can always add your own ideas to your drawings to make them even more fun.

Do you have a pencil and paper ready? Great! Let's start drawing.

Bird

There are many different kinds of birds. Some are big, like the ostrich that can grow as tall as 9 feet (3 m). Others are small, like hummingbirds that are only a few inches long. We're going to draw a mama bird and a baby bird in a nest.

Begin by drawing a pointy head and a skinny neck.

Add a straight back and a triangle-shaped tail.

Now, draw a rounded chest and backside.

Add a little wing.

Let's add a baby bird.
Draw a round head
and add a beak that
looks like the letter "M"
tilted to the side.

Add a "dot" eye
and a skinny neck.

A quick way to draw the
nest is to make lots of
crisscross lines—sort
of like the letter "X."

Add a few eggs to complete your drawing. What do you
think the baby bird is saying to its mama?

Cat

Cats have eyes that are especially good for seeing when there's not much light. But did you know that cats can't see things that are right under their noses? That's why they sometimes don't see the little treats you put on the floor in front of them.

You can draw a cat if you follow these steps:

Draw a triangle nose, a little "beard," and two puffy cheeks. Now add some round eyes and draw straight lines inside the eyes.

Cats have great hearing. Give your cat some big ears and a fuzzy head. Add whiskers, too.

The next thing your cat needs is a round back and two front legs. Add some fur under the head to make the chest fuzzy.

The last step is to add a back leg and a long tail. Don't forget to draw a little bit of the back leg on the other side, too. Add some zigzag lines for fur on the kitty's tummy.

Dog

We all know that dogs have a better sense of smell than humans do—but how much better? BZZZZZ! Sorry, you're out of time! The answer is 1,000 times better!

We'll start drawing our cartoon dog by making a triangle nose. Now add some rounded lines for the area near the mouth.

Draw a tongue and two big, round eyes.

This is one way to draw the ears. You can experiment with the ears by making them longer or shorter.

Your dog needs a long, straight back and a tail. You can also give your dog a little round backside.

Add two legs and feet. Notice how each paw has some lines on it to show the toes.

The last step is to add two more legs and two feet on the other side.

Since these legs and feet are partially hidden by the legs closest to us, you only have to draw part of the other two legs and feet.

Is this little guy cute or what?

Look! He's happy to see you! He's wagging his tail.

Guess who just had a bath? This is what happens when you dry your dog with a blow dryer.

Hmmm...Looks like somebody is hungry.

Alligator

We'll start by drawing an alligator. Alligators have strong muscles that snap their jaws shut. But the muscles that open their mouths are very weak. It's easy to hold their mouths shut. Just don't let go!

Begin your gator by drawing the nostrils and a bumpy snout.

Add the top of the mouth.

Now we need some big, round eyes.

Draw a curved line from below the front of the snout to the back of the right eye.

Now add the back. Just draw some zigzags.

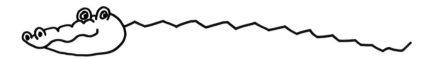

The next step is to add short, fat legs and a chest.

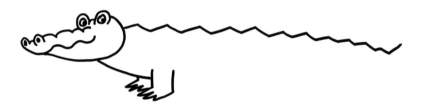

Draw a stomach and some more short, fat legs.

Connect a line from the back leg to the top of the tail.

For a finishing touch, you can add some scales and some lines on the gator's stomach.

You can also hide your alligator in the water...

Or you can draw your alligator chasing some dinner.

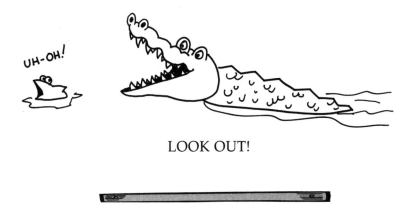

UH-OH!

LOOK OUT!

Turtle

There are more than 250 species of turtle, but you've probably never seen one like the one you're about to draw.

Begin by drawing a head and neck.

Next, add eyes and a shell.

Your turtle needs four legs and a tail. Add them now.

Draw some shapes on your turtle's shell. Add toenails, too.

Here's how to draw a turtle sleeping.

Do you know what kind of turtle this is?

Right! It's a snapping turtle!

Monkey

Monkeys belong to a group of animals called primates. Primates include monkeys, apes, and another really weird group of creatures called humans. That's right! People are primates, too.

To draw a monkey, start with a face that looks a little like a three-leaf clover. Add eyes, nostrils, and a mouth. Notice that the mouth turns up a little in the middle.

Add a lot of fur around the face.

Before you draw this next step, notice the shape of the line. There's a long curvy line for the monkey's back. At the bottom of the back, the line curves back the other way to form the monkey's tail. Take another good look. Okay? Ready to draw?

Draw the monkey's back and tail.

Now it's time to draw the monkey's leg. It looks a little like a human leg. The foot is long and it has long toes. Also add a short line above the leg for the monkey's arm.

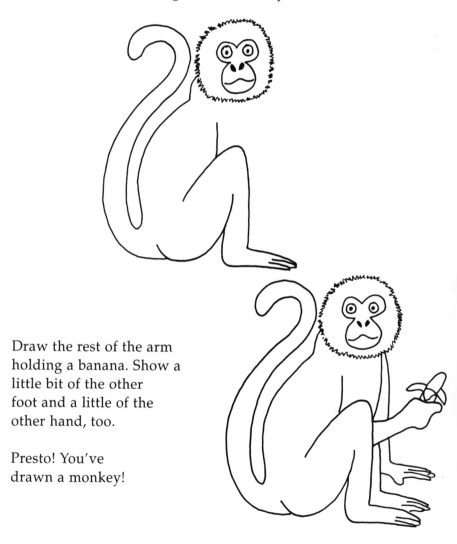

Draw the rest of the arm holding a banana. Show a little bit of the other foot and a little of the other hand, too.

Presto! You've drawn a monkey!

Mouse

Mice are curious little creatures. They usually come out at night and explore the area near their nests. Even though people think of mice as eating a lot of cheese, their favorite foods are cereal grains and seeds. Here's how to draw a mouse:

Draw the nose, eyes, and ears.

Add a round back.

Now your mouse needs short legs and pointy toes...

And a long, long tail.

EEEK! A mouse!
If you draw a mouse hole with part of the mouse peeking out, you get a cute cartoon.

Here's the same idea using a piece of cheese. The mouse is thinking, "Yum!"

Answers

Quicksolve Whodunits

Jilted Joker. Minutes before, the clown had a bunch of helium-filled balloons. He did not have them when he was discovered. He must have let them go—after he tied the derringer to them. The evidence flew away!

Skating Rink Robbery. Frank said he heard a noise from the soundproof office while he was in the main room with the loud music.

Burglars and Bludgeons. Mr. Bludgeon was caught for speeding north of the cabin, apparently running away from town and the telephones into the wilderness.

Smith and Smith, Ex-Partners. He wanted to see if Mr. Smith's shoes were wet. If they were, he must have sneaked in the back door to surprise his partner and kill him, and Dr. Quicksolve would have solved another case, because, coming through the garage, they would be dry. They were. He had. He did.

Made in the Shades. She described the man as having blue eyes, yet he approached her only after he put sunglasses on. She could not have seen the color of his eyes!

Postal Clown. Although the footprints were too small for Soapy to have made them with his feet, he could have attached a smaller pair of shoes to his stilts to make the tracks and create false evidence. Dr. Quicksolve wanted to look for the shoes and stilts.

Dit Dah Dilemma. The lines in the dirt are the Morse code pattern for S-A-M. Apparently, Mr. Graff was trying to tell who shot him without being too obvious to the killer, who may have seen what he did.

Brainteasers

1. The number of passing grades is a whole number less than 32, and 5 percent of it is also a whole number. The answer can only be 20. If 20 is the number of passing grades, the number of students from New York who took the test is one.

2. There is only one winner, so the remaining 110 players were defeated in 110 matches. Therefore, they used 110 balls.

3. Two glasses. Pick up the second glass, pour its contents into the ninth glass, and put it back. Then pick up the fourth glass, pour its contents into the seventh glass and put it back. Note that the seventh and ninth glasses are not moved.

4. Three ducks.

5. The reaction of the air that the little bird is pushing down in order to fly will partially affect both the dish of the scale and the floor of the room. The scale will show one pound minus some portion of the 5 ounces that the bird weighs. If the cage were sealed, the air would affect only the dish of the scale, and the scale would continue to read one pound.

6. Friday.

7. To "sint" means to take off your clothes, and to "sant" means to go into the water to bathe.

8. The parrot was deaf.

9. I spoke to Peter. If a person always lies or alternately, always tells the truth, he cannot admit that he is lying (if this person were a liar, he would be telling the truth, and if he were honest, he would be lying). Therefore, Paul could not have answered my question. Peter could answer about Paul without contradicting himself. What we still don't know is who the liar is.

10. 22 steps. While the Professor goes up the entire staircase, I descend the staircase except for 11 steps (7 at the top + 4 at the bottom). Since he goes twice as fast as I do, the entire staircase is 2 x 11 steps.

11. Thursday. The snake is lying, because it says that today is Saturday and tomorrow is Wednesday. Therefore today is one of the days when the snake lies (Tuesday, Thursday, or Saturday). It cannot be Saturday, or else the snake would not be lying in one statement. Nor can it be Tuesday for the same reason. It can only be Thursday.

12. One.

13. The blonde woman killed Arthur Farnanski. There are only four true statements. Only one person is guilty. Therefore three of the "I'm innocent" statements are true. Only one more statement can be true, and this must be the one made by the man in the dark suit or the one made by the blonde woman. Therefore, "The brunette killed him" and "One of the men killed him" are false statements, so the blonde woman is the killer.

14. Suppose a regular donut has 100 calories. If a low-calorie donut has 95 percent fewer calories, it must have 5 calories. Therefore you must eat 20 low-calorie donuts to get as many calories as you'd get from one regular donut.

15. Here is the code for the four men and their wives. M1 and W1 for the first man and wife; M2 and W2 for the second man and wife; M3 and W3 for the third; and M4 and W4 for the fourth.

> 1st crossing: M1 and W1 cross, M1 returns.
> 2nd crossing: M2 and W2 cross, M2 returns.
> 3rd crossing: M1 and M2 cross, M2 and W2 return.
> 4th crossing: W2 and W3 cross, M1 returns.
> 5th crossing: M1 and M2 cross, W3 returns.
> 6th crossing: M3 and M4 cross, M3 returns.
> 7th crossing: M3 and W3 cross, M4 returns.
> 8th crossing: M4 and W4 cross.

16. The stationary machine makes three waffles per second. If you had four stationary machines, you'd be making 12 waffles per second. The portable machine makes 120 waffles per minute, which is the same as two per second. To produce 12 waffles per second, you would need $12/2 = 6$ portable machines.

17. The father is 41 and the son is 14.

18. The minimum number of parts that could have been left is 3 (the link that is cut and the two disconnected parts of the chain). The maximum number will be 5, as shown in the figure below.

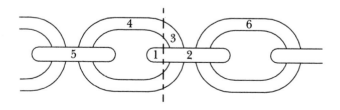

19. Jones did worse than Smith, even after Smith's second 60 percent loss. To see why, assume that each man started with $1,000. Jones ended up with $150, following his 85 percent loss. Smith had $400 after his first loss. After his second loss, he had $240 less, for a total of $160.

20. The reward was $125. If you erase 1, you have 25 left, which is one-fifth the original amount. If you erase 2, you have 5 left, which is one-fifth of this amount.

To get 125, find a two-digit number in which you can take the first digit off and have the result be one-fifth of the number. The only possible number is 25. 25 x 5 = 125.

Index